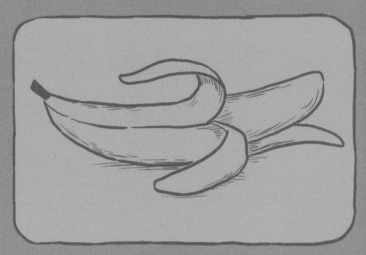

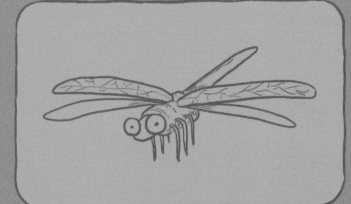

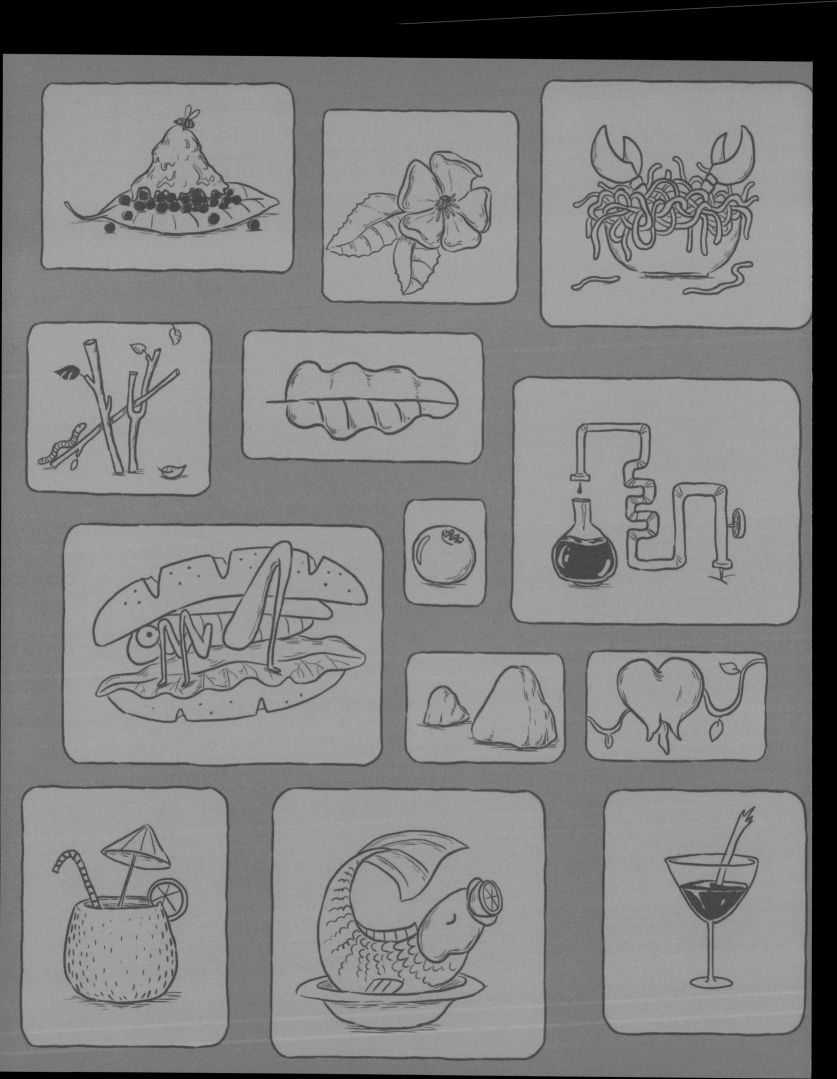

DO FISH GO FISHING?

How Animals Eat

ALBATROS

DO FISH GO FISHING?
How Animals Eat

Written by Petra Bartíková & Illustrated by Katarína Macurová

How PLATYPUSES eat

It's still not enough food. I'm really hungry!

THEY LIVE ON LAND AND IN WATER.

THEY ARE AT HOME IN PONDS AND POOLS IN EASTERN AUSTRALIA.

HOW STRANGE!
WHILE PLATYPUSES ARE MAMMALS, MEANING THEIR OFFSPRING DRINK THE MOTHER'S MILK, THEY HATCH FROM EGGS LIKE BIRDS.

Daily special

- ROAST INSECT LARVAE
- RAGU FROM MEATY WORMS
- STUFFED CRAYFISH

A TRULY UNIQUE ANIMAL.

IT'S THE ONLY ANIMAL ON EARTH THAT HAS THE BEAK OF A DUCK, THE FUR OF AN OTTER, AND LOOKS LIKE A BEAVER FROM A DISTANCE.

How FLEAS eat

THEY LIVE IN THE FUR OF ANIMALS AND DRINK THEIR BLOOD. WATCH OUT, THOUGH – THEY ALSO BITE PEOPLE!

This Bloody Mary tastes great, my dear.

THEY CAN DRINK AND CARRY MORE LIQUID THAN THEY ACTUALLY WEIGH.

LOOK AT THOSE **HUGE THINGS**

WHEN THEY MOVE THROUGH FUR AND MAKE A RUCKUS, ANIMALS SHAKE LIKE CRAZY.

FLEAS HAVE REALLY STRONG LEGS, THANKS TO THEIR BULKY THIGHS.

A-positive is the tastiest.

THEY HAVE HAIRS ON THEIR LEGS AND BODY THAT HELP THEM TRAVEL THROUGH REALLY **THICK FUR**.

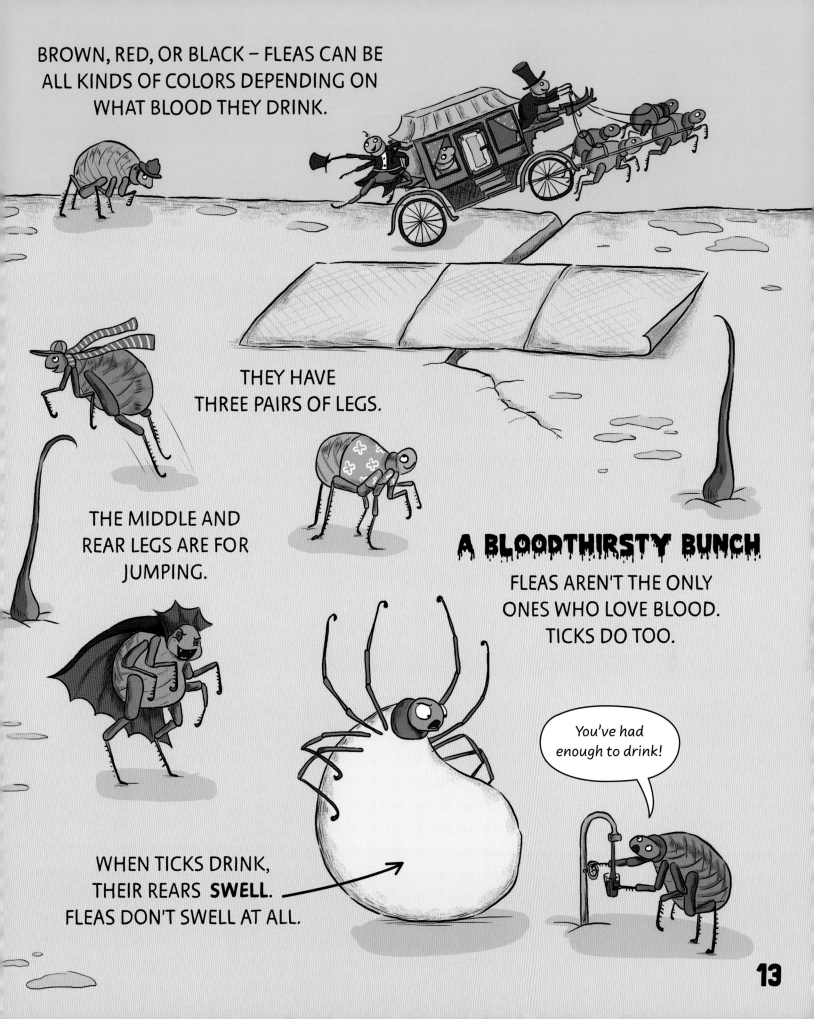

BROWN, RED, OR BLACK – FLEAS CAN BE ALL KINDS OF COLORS DEPENDING ON WHAT BLOOD THEY DRINK.

THEY HAVE THREE PAIRS OF LEGS.

THE MIDDLE AND REAR LEGS ARE FOR JUMPING.

A BLOODTHIRSTY BUNCH

FLEAS AREN'T THE ONLY ONES WHO LOVE BLOOD. TICKS DO TOO.

WHEN TICKS DRINK, THEIR REARS **SWELL**. FLEAS DON'T SWELL AT ALL.

You've had enough to drink!

How CHIMPANZEES eat

THEY LIVE IN THE AFRICAN SAVANNAS AND RAINFORESTS.

WHEN THEY FIND AN ANT COLONY, THEY TAKE A BRANCH AND STICK IT INSIDE . . .

THEY TAKE CARE OF THEIR RELATIVES AND SHARE GOODIES THEY FIND IN THE FOREST.

THEN THEY SIMPLY PULL OUT THE TWIG, AND LICK ALL THE ANTS OFF.

Wee!

THEY START LOOKING FOR SOMETHING GOOD TO EAT AS SOON AS THEY WAKE UP.

THEY LOVE TO JUMP FROM TREE TO TREE.

THEY ARE SUPER SMART AND USE DIFFERENT KINDS OF TOOLS.

THEY LIKE TO EAT SWEET FRUIT THE MOST, BUT ALSO ENJOY JUICY LEAVES, BLOSSOMS, RESIN, SOFT BARK, AND SEEDS.

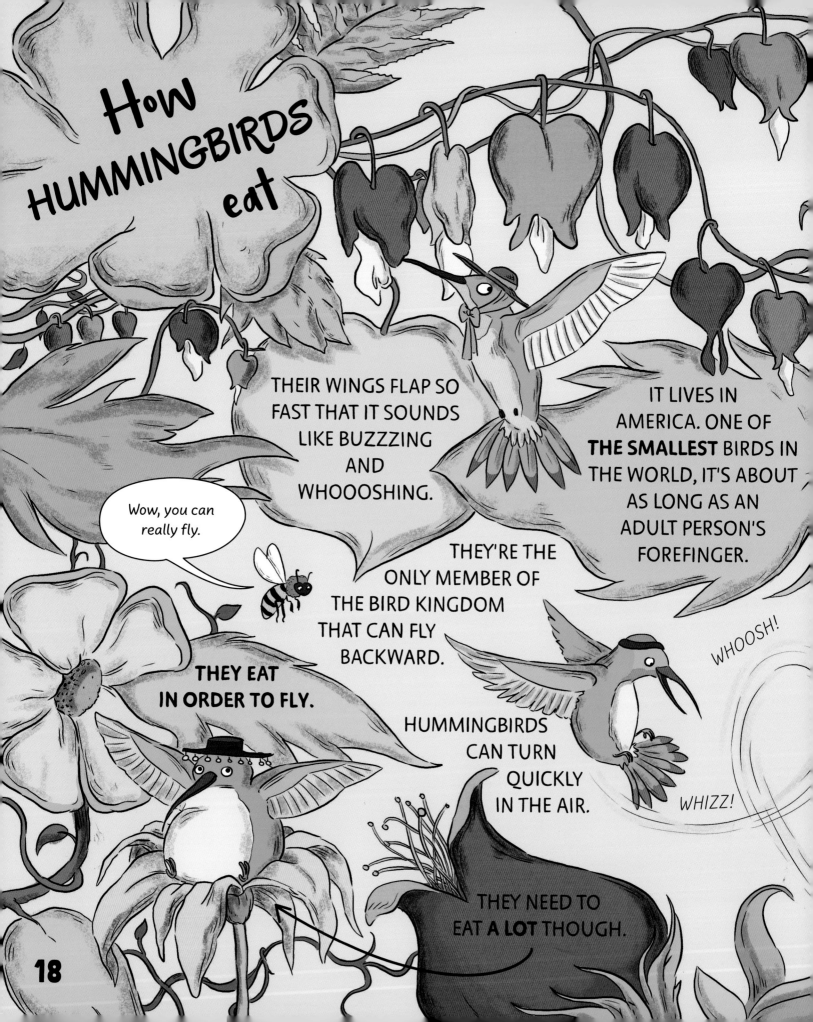

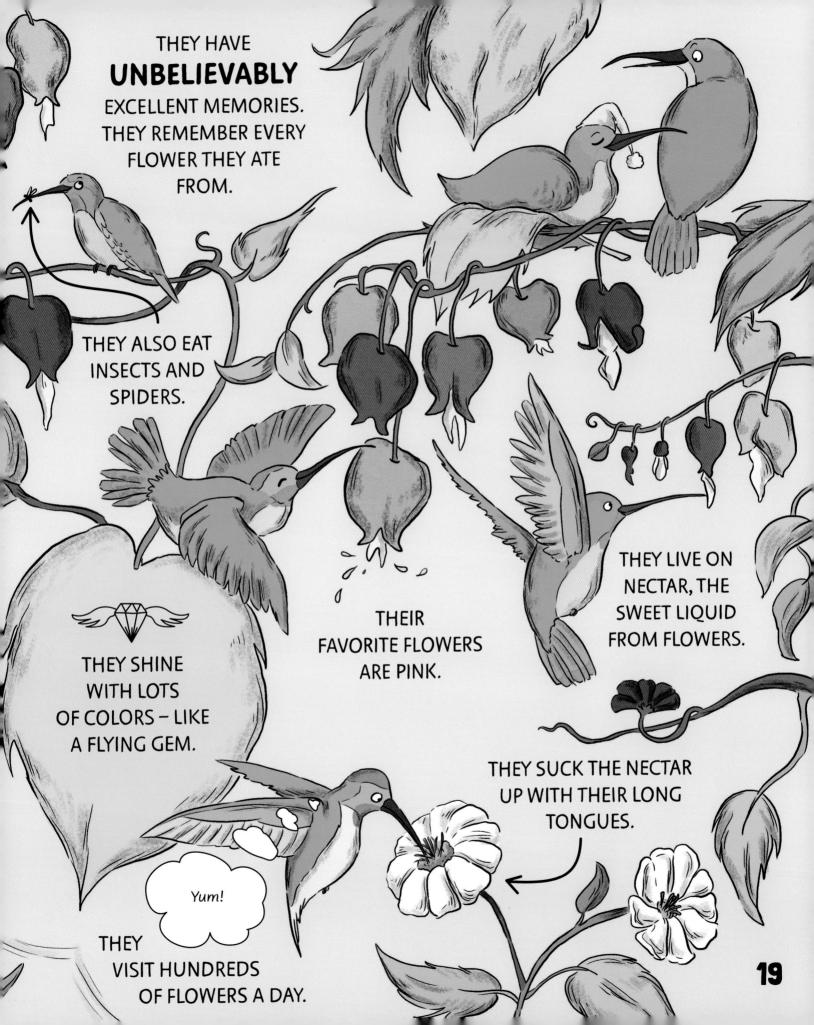

23

... OR MADE UP OF SEVERAL DROPPING STUCK TOGETHER.

THEY CAN RUN FASTER UPHILL THAN DOWNHILL...

BECAUSE THEIR FRONT LEGS ARE **SHORTER** THAN THEIR REAR LEGS.

THEY EAT VARIOUS KINDS OF GRASS, SPROUTS, AND JUICY HERBS.

THEY HAVE **LONG** EARS. AND EXCELLENT HEARING!

She's listening to pop music and jazz at the same time.

Which does she dance to?

THEY **CHEW ON** BRANCHES IN THE WINTER AND ON BUDS IN THE SPRING.

© B4U Publishing for Albatros,
an imprint of Albatros Media Group, 2024
5. května 1746/22, Prague 4, Czech Republic

Author: Petra Bartíková
Illustrator: Katarína Macurová
Editor: Scott Alexander Jones

www.albatrosbooks.com

Printed in China by Leo Paper Group.

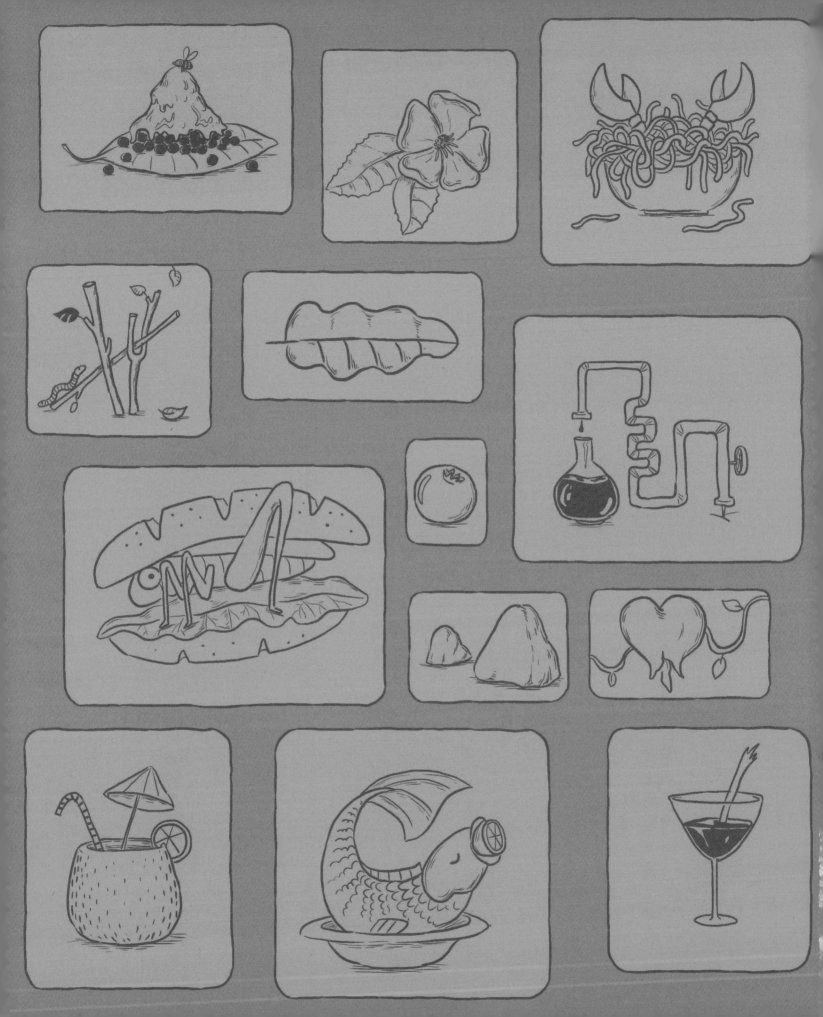